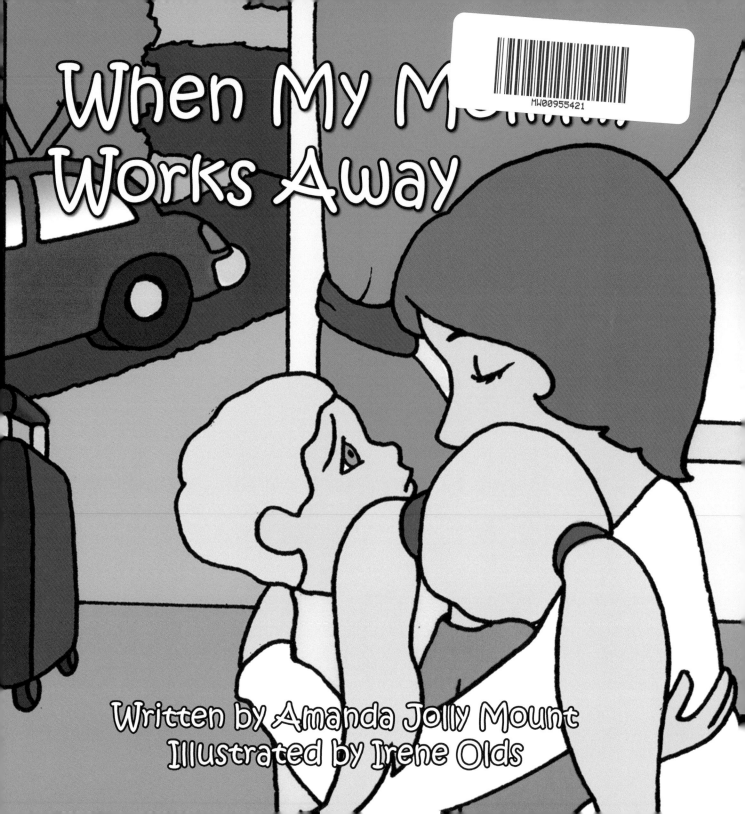

When My Mommy Works Away

Written by Amanda Jolly Mount
Illustrated by Irene Olds

When My Mommy Works Away

Written by Amanda Jolly Mount
Illustrated by Irene Olds

Dedicated to Helen and Kenny

AuthorHouse™
1663 Liberty Drive
Bloomington, IN 47403
www.authorhouse.com
Phone: 1-800-839-8640

Published by AuthorHouse 03/02/2012

ISBN: 978-1-4567-9494-1 (sc)

Library of Congress Control Number: 2012900145

Any people depicted in stock imagery provided by Thinkstock are models,
and such images are being used for illustrative purposes only.
Certain stock imagery © Thinkstock.

This book is printed on acid-free paper.

authorHOUSE®

My Mommy leaves me safe at home
Where I am never left alone

See all the places she may go

My Mommy thinks of me when she's away
All throughout her busy day

Maybe a week, maybe a day

CPSIA information can be obtained
at www.ICGtesting.com
Printed in the USA
LVIC06n0826210617
538847LV00017B/461

* 9 7 8 1 4 5 6 7 9 4 9 4 1 *